Bob Chilcott

Jazz Folk Songs
for Choirs

9 songs from around the world
for mixed voices and jazz trio or piano solo

MUSIC DEPARTMENT

OXFORD
UNIVERSITY PRESS

OXFORD
UNIVERSITY PRESS

Great Clarendon Street, Oxford OX2 6DP, England
198 Madison Avenue, New York, NY 10016, USA

Oxford University Press is a department of the University of Oxford.
It furthers the University's aim of excellence in research, scholarship,
and education by publishing worldwide

Music origination by Enigma Music Production Services, Amersham, Bucks.
Printed in Great Britain on acid-free paper by
Halstan & Co. Ltd., Amersham, Bucks.

Contents

Composer's note

When I was a choir and ensemble singer I always loved to perform pieces influenced by jazz. The style creates a real sense of energy and presents an interesting choral challenge in terms of blend, intonation, rhythm, phrasing, and making often well-known songs sound natural and true. In this book I have taken nine folk-song tunes and tried to create a palette of different jazz-influenced styles and colours that I hope choirs will enjoy working at. The songs can be performed by choir and piano, or by choir and jazz trio (piano, bass, and drums), and other instruments could also be added to the ensemble. The piano parts work well as notated in the book, but many players might like to improvise and solo, which would be fine too.

Structurally, most of the songs work best if performed as written. However, there is the opportunity in both 'Tuoll' on mun kultani' and 'Waltzing Matilda' to include a repeated section for solo instrumentalists or scat singers; instructions are written in the score. The Andalusian song 'En la Macarenita' was written for the inspirational Cuban vocal group Novel Voz, which is lucky enough to have within its ranks a singer who is wonderful at beatboxing, or vocal percussion. These kinds of effects would work really well in this song, should a member of the choir be willing to give them a go!

I would like to thank the editors Robyn Carpenter and Mary Chandler for their work on this volume, and also the pianist Alex Hawkins for his annotation of the bass parts and for playing on the backing CD (included with the spiral-bound edition) with Michael Chilcott and Derek Scurll.

Bob Chilcott, June 2008

for Jon Washburn and the Vancouver Chamber Choir

À la claire fontaine
(There by the crystal fountain)

English version BC

Trad. French Canadian
arr. BOB CHILCOTT

S. J'ai per-du mon a-mi-e sans l'a-voir mé-ri-té,
I lost my on-ly lov-er and still I don't know why,

T. J'ai per-du mon a-mi-e sans l'a-voir mé-ri-
I lost my lov-er and still I don't know

pour un bou-quet de ro-ses que je lui re-fu-sais.
All for a bunch of ro-ses; that I can-not de-ny.

-té, pour un bou-quet de ro-ses, de ro-ses.
why, for a bunch of ro-ses, of ro-ses.

S. Il y a long-temps que je t'ai-me, ja-mais je ne t'ou-blie-rai,
How can I be-gin to for-get you? Time can't stop me lov-ing you.

A. *div.*
oo

T.
B.
oo

Il   y   a   long-temps que je t'ai – me,   ja – mais   je   ne t'ou – blie – rai.
How   can I   be – gin   to for – get   you?   Time   can't stop me lov – ing   you.

for Novel Voz

En la Macarenita
(Down in the Macarena)

English version BC

Trad. Andalusian
arr. BOB CHILCOTT

*Omit bracketed notes as required.

for Lizzie Maclean

Hush, little baby

Trad. American
arr. BOB CHILCOTT

for the Japan Choral Association

Sakura
(Cherry tree)

Trad. Japanese
arr. BOB CHILCOTT

English version BC

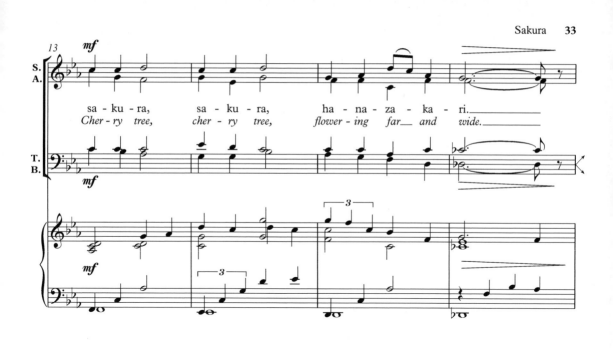

sa - ku - ra,   sa - ku - ra,   ha - na - za - ka - ri.
Cher - ry   tree,   cher - ry   tree,   flower - ing   far   and   wide.

mp cantabile

f espress.   *mf dolce*   *mp*

poco rit.   **a tempo**

p

Sa - ku - ra, sa - ku - ra, ya - yo - i no so - ra___ wa
Cher - ry tree, cher - ry tree, spreads as far as you can___ see,

Sa - ku - ra, sa - ku - ra, ya - yo - i no so - ra___
Cher - ry tree, cher - ry tree, spreads as far as you can___

Sa - ku - ra, sa - ku - ra, ya - yo - i no so - ra wa___
Cher - ry tree, cher - ry tree, spreads as far as you can see,___

mi - wa - ta - su ka - gi - ri, ka - su - mi ka ku - mo___ ka
nes - tled in the arms of___ spring, in a mist that pas - ses___ by,

wa mi - wa - ta - su ka - gi - ri, ka - su - mi ka ku - mo ka
see, nes - tled in the arms of spring, in a mist that pas - ses by,

mi - wa - ta - su ka - gi - ri, ka - su - mi ka ku - mo ka
nes - tled in the arms of spring, in a mist that pas - ses by,

for Justin Doyle and the Ryedale Festival

Scarborough Fair

Trad. English
arr. BOB CHILCOTT

for Jon Washburn and the Vancouver Chamber Choir

Tell my ma

Children's song from Northern Ireland
arr. BOB CHILCOTT

for Waverley Care and its work supporting those in Scotland whose lives are touched by HIV

The House of the Rising Sun

Trad. American
arr. BOB CHILCOTT

done,_____ Tell her to shun____ that house____ in New____ Or - leans,_____

_____ They   call____   the Ris - ing_ Sun.

If I'd-a list-ened____   what____ my ma - ma_ said,   I'd-a

Go - in'___ to spend___ the rest   of   my life,_____   Be -

- neath___ the Ris - ing Sun,_____   be - neath__ the Ris - ing

Sun,_____   be - neath__ the Ris - ing Sun.

Tuoll' on mun kultani
(There is my loved one)

Trad. Finnish
arr. BOB CHILCOTT

English version BC

Voi__ mi-nun kul - ta-ni, voi mi-nun lin - tu-ni, kun et tu - le jo,__
Ah__ you, my loved one,__ ah you, my dear one,__ still you do not come,__

kun et tu - le jo!_____
still you do not come!_____

kun et tu - le jo!_____ mm_____
still you do not come!_____ mm_____

kun et tu - le jo!_____ mm____
still you do not come!_____ mm____

Lin - nut ne lau - la-vat so - ri - al - la suul - la, so - ri - am-pi kul - ta - ni
Hear - ing the song_ of the birds_ high a - bove me Fills me with the hope that you

ää - ni on kuul - la. Voi mi-nun kul - ta-ni, voi mi-nun lin - tu-ni,
real - ly could love me. Ah you, my loved one,_ ah you, my dear one,_

kun et tu - le jo,   kun et tu - le   jo!_____
still you do not come,   *still you do not   come!*_____   *mm*___

(optional instrumental repeat)*

mp poco cresc.

S.   mm_____   ah_____

A.   mm_____   ah_____

T.   ah_____

B.

(optional instrumental repeat)*

mp poco cresc.

*If the repeat is made the choir should re-enter at bar 23.

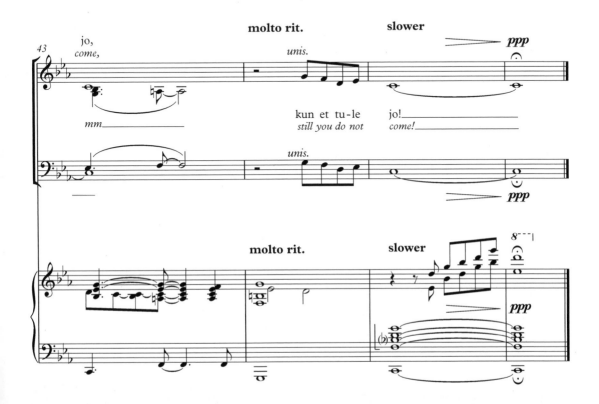

for Justin Doyle and the Dorking Choral Society

Waltzing Matilda

A. B. 'Banjo' Paterson (1864–1941)

Trad. Australian
arr. BOB CHILCOTT

sang as he sat and wait-ed till his bil-ly boiled,

'Who'll come a-waltz-ing Ma - til - - da with me?'

sang   as__ he shoved   that__ jum-buck   in__ his tuck-er - bag,_____

'You'll   come a-waltz-ing Ma - til - - da with me.'_____

Who's that jol - ly jum - buck you've got in your tuck-er - bag,

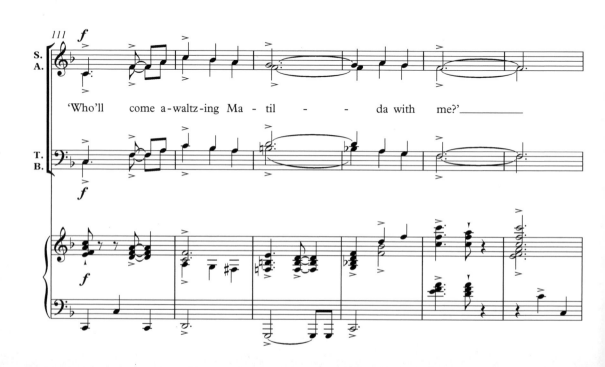

'Who'll come a-waltz-ing Ma - til - - da with me?'

you'll come a - waltz - ing Ma - til - da with me.'

And his

ghost may be heard as you pass by the bil-la - bong,

CD track list and credits

The CD included with the spiral-bound edition of *Jazz Folk Songs for Choirs* (ISBN 978-0-19-336182-9) contains jazz-trio backings for the seven accompanied songs in the collection and a pronunciation guide for each of the foreign-language texts.

Track list

Jazz-trio backings:

1. À la claire fontaine
2. Sakura
3. Scarborough Fair
4. Tell my ma
5. The House of the Rising Sun
6. Tuoll' on mun kultani
7. Waltzing Matilda

Foreign-language poems:

8. À la claire fontaine (French)
9. La Macarenita (Spanish)
10. Sakura (Japanese)
11. Tuoll' on mun kultani (Finnish)

CD credits

Piano: Alexander Hawkins
Bass: Michael Chilcott
Drums: Derek Scurll

French speaker: Agnès Ausseur
Spanish speaker: Karen Fodor
Japanese speaker: Hidemi Hatada
Finnish speaker: Silja Murto

Recorded on 29 April 2008 at the Royal College of Music Studios, London, by Stephen Harrington. Mastered by Tim Turan at Turan Audio.